Wise Up, O Man of God

Written by Laurie De Seguirant

PublishAmerica
Baltimore

First printing

ISBN: 1-60610-941-3
PUBLISHED BY PUBLISHAMERICA, LLLP
www.publishamerica.com
Baltimore

Printed in the United States of America

Jen—

May God richly
bless your service!

Laurie

INTRODUCTION

There appears to be a trend, and perhaps popular pastime for some "historians" within our halls of higher education, to denigrate the memory of our forefathers. History now reads like the pages of a grocery-stand gossip column. I have to ask myself— why? Aren't these professors dedicated to truth? Isn't this, in its purest form, an endeavor to set straight history as it really happened? Or are there actually individuals seeking to vilify men who have long been lauded as heroic? Perhaps this new scholarly review is motivated by something far more insidious. Perhaps, seeing that man and the message are so closely connected, they have surmised that by attacking the man's character, the core values [attributed to the Almighty] that made this country great will accompany the man in his historical decay.

Ah, but let's not rush to conclusions. We might find that in their effort to remove any notion of our forefathers' regard for the Almighty, these professors of higher learning have become snared by their own teaching.

Let us, for the moment, look at our forefathers according to today's historical revision. We will not be inspired by exploits colorfully brushed upon canvas, nor by the steadfast marble statues portraying majestic images. We will not laud them as did their contemporary writers. Let us look at them as men— mere men. Let us see them as many of today's professors would like for us to see them: with darkened hearts, feet of clay, despised by those who knew them best.

Having stripped these men of any cause for adulation, let us ask the wise professor what [then] made this nation great? If not by the frailty of man, what? All that remains is their message; their message and majesty of Almighty God! And so, let us, by the very testimony of these historical revisionists, disregard for the moment the greatness of man and let us simply focus upon the promise of God.

Based upon their argument, we do not need the giants of yesterday to set our nation right. We need only men and women with burdened hearts and feet of clay, who often feel alone, to individually give God His rightful place in their lives. For this nation to rise again, God must once again be elevated to His rightful place as the Rock of Ages!

Wise Up, O Man of God!

"If my people who are called by my name shall humble themselves and pray, and seek my face and turn from their wicked ways then will I hear from heaven and will forgive their sins and will heal their land." 2 Chronicles 7:14.

PREFACE

*"I take full responsibility; I'm the one you've been looking for—the one who let the world change. I allowed situational ethics to replace responsibility, political correctness to become the national language, pornography to replace true art, lawlessness—freedom and religious leaders—God. That's right; if you ever wonder why the world has changed, I'm the guy—***guilty, your honor, guilty as charged!"***

You see, I grew up in the *good old days* when we still had classroom fingernail inspections, stood in unison when an adult entered the room, recited the pledge of allegiance without fear of hurting someone's feelings, shopped on Saturday because Sunday the stores were closed, played outside after dark, told our moms we were walking to a friend's house and never gave a thought about our safe return, ate dinner with our families, left the doors unlocked, went to drive-in movies, wore bleached white socks with polished shoes, always tucked in our shirts, made certain our cuffs were folded the same, sat with our families in church, and said prayers before going to bed. It was a different world and somehow I let it slip away.

It wasn't an act of terrorism; no foreign army invaded my country. I just—gave it up. Fighting for its moral culture, its Judeo-Christian foundation, a world view of right and wrong, black and white, was simply too time-consuming. Let someone else worry about that. After all, I am a Christian. I am in God's hands, sort of a celestial insurance broker with an ultimate fire insurance rider on the side.

Uh, excuse me? How much will have to happen before we Christians get off of our blessed ass-urance and realize that redemption comes with responsibility?

Allow me to be blunt. This is a call to arms! This is a call to the pious preacher who has beat his pulpit to splinters for twenty years and hasn't had a word from the Carpenter for about as long. This is for the weak-kneed defeatist Christians who are counting on tomorrow being worse than today—and wouldn't accept a blessing from God if He drove up in a pizza delivery truck during *Monday Night Football* and delivered it Himself. "Hope" would devastate their lust to wallow in despair. This is for the man, woman, boy and girl who is willing, even if just for a moment, to consider the possibility that there is still one more spiritual awakening yet to come on God's celestial calendar. Mark you calendar, Christian, the time is **NOW!**

There is a spiritual battle on the horizon. On which side will you serve? Someone once asked, "If you were arrested for being a Christian—would there be enough evidence to convict you?" Who are you when there is no one but you and God in the room?

There must be a standard, a starting point from which our discussion begins. It is my opinion that this standard must be the Bible. I am not interested in debating its authenticity and its relevance. I recognize that many continue to debate whether it IS God's word or it ISN'T God's Word. And if the Bible IS the Word of God, is it the "total" Word of God or does it simply "contain" the Word of God?

Personally, I believe its original text is wholly the inspired Word of God. It is my personal belief that as God breathed His Word; His chosen, individual writers penned those precious and precise words. I am confident that the Bible has been miraculously protected, enduring years of translation and interpretation to hold intact within its pages everything God intended for us to know of His love for us. It is, however, humanly impossible to prove the validity of the Bible, so fellow Christian, STOP TRYING! Read it, live it, share it, but stop trying to cram it down your neighbor's throat. Creation cannot add one iota of credibility to the Creator. The Creator is, who the Creator is, regardless of the vain attempts of humanity to explain (or explain away) the truth of the Creator.

The Bible can only be proclaimed as the sole truth by its content and focus upon the one, true Word of God, Jesus Christ. John 1:4 emphasizes this transformation: *"and the WORD was made FLESH and dwelt among us."*

There is no need for human authority to attempt to prove it; there is, however, a great need for a humble and redeemed humanity TO LIVE IT!

This book is for individuals who have come to a point in their lives where they are willing to be truthful with themselves and with God. They are willing to say, "I don't have all the answers and I don't believe my church or minister does either. I can't say for certain which things I truly believe and which I have been manipulated into believing. I am not certain I understand what a real personal relationship with Almighty God is; I'm just praying **He grades on a big curve!**"

Sound at all like you? Well if not, read further anyway; I'll probably use you as an example!

IF MY PEOPLE ARE CALLED BY MY NAME...

God's blessing is not conditional or dependent upon the universal revival of every living soul. Conversely, the security of a nation is greatly dependent upon God's children and their attitude towards Him. God is not a celestial real estate agent. The United States of America has not been blessed because of its land value. Our nutrient and mineral rich soil did not influence the Almighty. Our prime location, latitude and longitude, was not a factor in God's blessing. Our mountains, lakes, rivers, soaring redwoods, majestic canyons, expansive wilderness and thriving cities did not captivate the investment speculation of an Almighty God.

So why the U.S.A.?

In his message entitled "The Great Revival," James P. Wesberry describes the prayer room of the nation's capitol. It houses ten chairs, two kneeling benches, and a beautiful altar with an open Bible pointing to Psalm 16:1: *"Preserve me, O God: for in Thee do I put my trust."*

Above the open Bible is a stained glass window. The window speaks of the religious faith of our nation. George Washington, the father of our country, is on his knees, reminding us of the words from his first inaugural speech, in which he said:

"It would be peculiarly improper to omit the first official act, my fervent supplications to that Almighty Being who rules over the universe, who presides in the councils of nations, and whose providential aids can supply every human defect, that His benediction may consecrate to the liberties and happiness of the people of the United States, a government, instituted by themselves for these essential purposes, and may enable every instrument employed in its administration to execute with success the functions allotted to His charge."

Above and below are the two sides of the Great Seal of the United States. Above is a pyramid and eye with the Latin phrases, "God has favored our undertakings," and "A Unum," meaning "One from many." Under the seal is a phrase from Lincoln's immortal Gettysburg Address: "This nation under God."

Why the U.S.A.?

The United States of America has enjoyed God's blessing because our forefathers recognized Almighty God as the creator and they chose to build their new nation upon the Rock of Ages!

God's influence upon this nation is witnessed in our most precious documents. It has been etched in granite walls and spoken in the oath of office. And yet there are those who would remove any reference to the Almighty from our schools, businesses, courtrooms, currency and conversation. And at the first sign of national disaster or unrest they point an accusing finger at the Christian and cry, "Where is your God?"

Excuse me, but didn't you invite Him to leave?

It's time for Christians to rise above the strife by dropping to their knees and humbly inviting Him to return!

The United States of America is still [statistically] considered a Christian nation. Approximately 159 million people, 76.5% of the United States' population, consider themselves "Christian." There has, however, been a decline in recent years. Previously, the figure was 87% and stable. Nevertheless, 159 million is a staggering number! Why then, do we find our core values being uprooted? Think about that for a minute. What on earth is that power that causes the very children of God to recoil in fear? And if you smugly say, "The power of Satan"— BONG! You lose. Go to jail, do not collect any cash. The very Bible you piously carry to church each weekend boldly proclaims that WE are more than conquerors to Him that loves US! Satan gets a bad rap on that one. No; it is our own selfish fear—that part of us that is so desirous for applause, for acceptance, for love—that causes us to sit in our pews when called upon to take a stand in the streets!

So, whose are you? Are you part of the 159 million? If so, are you an active, vibrant part, or are you making certain no dust gathers on your favorite pew by keeping your posterior firmly positioned upon it? Did God command us to idly sit by and watch the world go to hell in a handbasket?

The first premise of Chronicles 7:14 is, "if My people..." Whose are you? Are you truly a man, woman or child of God? I know that Biblical scholars and theologians will rip me to shreds for what they might consider loose transliterations of the scripture. I realize this verse was spoken to the children of Israel but when God speaks to Israel, He often reveals principles He has set in place for all of creation. As I read it, this verse is directed to those He is specifically addressing in the beginning of the verse, **His people**. The success or failure of the promise in this verse is contingent upon **His people**. Who are they today? Are they those who feel that since they were born in America they are automatically Christian? An evangelist once commented that even if a person is born in a garage, it won't make that person a car.

The Old Testament refers to "God's people," Israel, over and over again. It would appear from the New Testament that Jesus intended to extend "God's people" to others outside the Jewish family:

"I am the good shepherd, and I know my sheep, and I am known of mine. As the Father knoweth me, even so I know the Father; and I lay down my life for the sheep. And OTHER SHEEP I have that are not of this fold; them also I must bring, and they shall hear my voice; and there shall be ONE FOLD and ONE SHEPHERD" John 10:14-16.

Jesus fulfilled this promise upon the cross of Calvary with a once-for-all atonement on mankind's behalf, by His substitutionary death. Victory over death was realized by His ultimate resurrection. Salvation is accomplished when individuals from any ethnicity, culture, religious background, political persuasion, sexual orientation, economic status or criminal background recognize their spiritual need and yield to God Spirit's call. There is no "dressing up" for Jesus; this is a "come as you are" party.

As a side note, I have always been sadly amused by those theologians who are compelled to spend countless hours arguing the topic of predestination, election, foreknowledge and free will. If the terms are foreign to you—count yourself fortunate!

But for the experimental "theologs" who might be reading, here's a simple theory for you. If a person recognizes his or her spiritual need, determines in their heart that Jesus died for them, asks to be a candidate for salvation by turning from their OWN WAY and yielding to God, GOD WILL ELECT THEM.

Let me address another Christian fallacy; the *fallacy of a personal Lord and Savior.*

WHAT? WHAT DO YOU MEAN—A **FALLACY**?

That's right, Christians. I am speaking directly to you for the moment. Now that I have caught your attention, let me explain. The definition of, "personal Lord and Savior" has lost its intended meaning. It no longer requires [our] being humbled by the realization that we are to be committed to a personal, daily, forever relationship—one in which we continually recognize our need and dependence upon Jesus for His love and direction. No longer does it reflect our awareness of His continual concern for our well-being and happiness.

Today, the term, "personal Lord and Savior" seems to have less to do with Christian commitment and more to do with Christian convenience. In other words, what I do with Him is my business—He is, after all, *"my"* personal Lord and Savior. He is there at *my* bidding to bless *my* desires, forgive *my* mistakes (PC cops require the elimination of "sin" in our vocabulary as it might offend someone) and otherwise grant *my* requests. He is, in fact, one of the many personal attachés in my life. Maybe you have some too: personal weight trainer, personal gardener, personal housekeeper, personal shopper, personal pet-sitter, personal banker, personal child care worker, personal travel agent, personal driver—why not a personal Lord and Savior to cap it all off?

Christian friend, what is your relationship right now to Jesus? Have you modified Him to conveniently fit your life? Or are you growing in grace and mercy to be the man or woman, boy or girl Jesus wants you to be? If indeed you ARE one of His people, called by his name, isn't it time to modify your wants and needs, your heart and life, to what He has planned for you?

The blessings of God will return to the nation when God's people recognize their responsibility, set aside their spiritual arrogance and humbly beseech Him and His divine presence. The survival of this nation, its culture, its Judeo-Christian concepts and traditions, its language and the sovereignty of its borders rests not so much upon the shoulders of every American, but rather upon on the knees of those who are the people of God. It is time we turn to the Great Physician who is able to heal the body, soul, mind and spirit. It is time we take a dose of His medicine to cure the self-inflicted disease of apathy. And it is high time we call it as it is. It is not, *"render unto Caesar the things that are Caesar's and unto God the things of God."* It is not the words of the children's hymn, *"This world is not my home—I'm just a passing through, my treasures are laid up somewhere beyond the blue."* It is not, *"Be ye separate from the world."* It isn't even, *"Ye are in the world but you are not of the world."* All of these have become excuses for Christians to disassociate themselves from the true mission of the church, and what is more, DO NOTHING in Jesus' name. It was never intended to be a "come and hear" Gospel. Jesus' command was always to "go and tell."

In Acts 1:8, moments before His ascension, Jesus said to his disciples:

"But you shall receive power—ability, efficiency and might—when the Holy Spirit has come upon you; and you shall be my witnesses in Jerusalem, and all Judea and Samaria and to the ends—the very bounds—of the earth!"

Where did Jesus want them to start? Jerusalem, right in their hometown.

I believe that before we can venture overseas to today's *"ends of the earth,"* we need to get our house, **AMERICA**, in order. We need to speak as one voice, neither liberal nor conservative, as it is too late and too serious a situation for partisan bickering. **ARE YOU ONE OF GOD'S PEOPLE**? If you say, "Yes, I am, and I am proud of it!" keep reading.

SHALL HUMBLE THEMSELVES

What does this phrase mean to you? Think about it for a second before reading on. What is true humility? What does it look like—how would I recognize it? What is it made of? Can it withstand the trials of life or does it wither? What is humility?

Unger's *Bible Dictionary* defines it like this:

"Christian humility is that grace which makes one think of himself no more highly than he ought to think (Romans 12:3). It requires us to feel that in God's sight we have no merit, and in honor to prefer our brethren to ourselves (Romans 12:10), but does not demand undue self-depreciation or depressing views of one's self, but lowliness of self-estimation, freedom from vanity. It is enjoined of God (Colossians 3:12; James 4:6). The word is about equivalent to meekness (Psalm 25:9) and is essential to discipleship to Christ (Matthew 18:3, 4)."

In essence, the word denotes not lowliness of character but an outcropping of Christian character, a self-induced lowliness of mind. It is not surprising that it follows so closely the outward expression of meekness. Picture, if you will, looking up at jagged cliffs rising from a tempestuous ocean. At the top of the cliff there appears movement. It is difficult to see at first, but as the clouds pass high overhead you clearly see the image of a muscular black stallion. Its coat glistens in the sun looking as if each tendon, each powerful muscle, strains to burst from its massive body! As you watch in total amazement its splendor, its beauty, its awesome power, the stallion rises upon its hind legs and kicks at the openness before him. And then you see it! It wasn't noticeable at first. You were so taken by this creature's beauty, its power, its majesty, that you almost missed it! Lodged within the stallion's jaws, there is a bit and bridle.

HEREIN IS THE DEFINITION OF HUMILITY! It is not the woe-is-me weak-kneed Christians who look as if they had been weaned on a dill pickle. It is not the habitual, "pray for me" Christian who fails to claim God's blessing because it might mean losing the attention so addictively desired and manipulatively received. It is not the "give God the glory" Christian who puts on a cloak of humility, as if it were a theater prop, only to accentuate and emphasize self. Friend, humility is simply POWER UNDER CONTROL! It is being who God made you to be—but letting Him control the reins. With that recognition one cannot help but be brought low. Not to be trod upon—but to live life where foot meets pavement, to the place where we are truly aware of the responsibility one has as a child of God, rather than thinking more highly of one's self or ones accomplishments. Not to have head hung low in shame, but to willingly bow to the Giver of life.

POWER UNDER CONTROL—Who controls the reins in your life?

You see, in reality, we are a powerful force with which to be reckoned. It is best that we do not recognize that power until we have given the reins to Him Who is the Author and Finisher of HIStory. When we do, we are powered not by desire and our strength, but He who lives within—and through us. And the life we now live, we live by faith, in adherence to and reliance upon, with complete trust in the Son of God, who loves us and gave Himself up for us.

So then how should we vote, with which political party should we associate—if at all? Give me a clean 'do and don't' list to follow.

We have an entire Book to follow; why not go to the Author for guidance?

PRAY

The previous section left us in a position of bowing to the Giver of life. It is not by coincidence that in such a position we make ready ourselves for the next requirement: **PRAYER**.

One need not be a Christian to realize that a certain amount of "meditation" is good for the soul. If a state of quiet nothingness is good for the soul, how much greater benefit when the heart and mind are in communication with God Almighty?

But is it really possible?

Have you ever had the feeling that praying to God was like tossing wishes into the air? Maybe you have experienced the "fast food prayer" that simply says, "OH GOD!"

Sad to say, I have been in prayer meetings where the pastor piously gets on his knees, followed by the elders in the church and anyone else wishing to participate, in what too often resembles theatrical blocking. I, too, have sat in a prayer circle, quietly rehearsing. I have prayed in the King James Version with the words, "Thee and Thou" placed properly within the context of my "spiritual script" so as to properly impress those with whom I recite. I therefore have a fairly good idea of what prayer—IS NOT.

So, what is prayer? Is it real communication? How do you do it effectively?

Frankly, if God knows everything...why does He need to hear about it from me, anyway?

Luke 11:1 records the following event:

"And it came to pass, that, as He was praying in a certain place, when He ceased, one of his disciples said unto him, Lord, teach us to pray, as John also taught his disciples."

Without doubt, these men had previously experienced some form of prayer in their lives, but there was something significantly different in the prayer of Jesus. His prayer was compelling! It was magnetic—alive, and the disciples instinctively knew that prayer was of vital importance to Jesus. They wanted that POWER to also be evident in their prayers.

Perhaps the following story will illustrate the mechanics of prayer. High winds caused a weekly prayer meeting to suffer an electrical outage. An electrician in the congregation, realizing that there was nothing he could do locally, called the station hub for information. They advised him that his immediate area had been affected but crews were already taking care of the situation. The service desk advised the electrician that the problem should be resolved in fifteen to twenty minutes. The gentleman quickly scribbled a note to the minister who, with no overhead lighting, was fast slipping into the shadows of sunset. The note simply said, "After prayer the power will return." How true it is! After prayer, the power always returns. Jesus' response holds within it the elements of Chronicles 7:14. Compare these two verses:

"If my people who are called by my name shall humble themselves and pray, and seek my face and turn from their wicked ways then will I hear from heaven and will forgive their sins and will heal their land." Chronicles 7:14

"When you pray say: [Our] Father, [Who is in heaven,] hallowed be Your name. Your kingdom come. Your will be done—held holy and revered—on earth as it is in heaven. Give us daily our bread (food for the morrow), and forgive us our sins, for we ourselves also forgive every one who is indebted to us—who has offended us or done us wrong; and bring us not into temptation, but rescue us from evil." Luke 11:2-4, *Amplified Bible.*

Jesus continues to teach the disciples the startling results of continual prayer as He shares with His disciples the parable of the friend who comes at midnight requesting three loaves of bread for an unexpected guest. A loose rendition of the event recorded in Luke goes something like this:

"What? It's midnight! I'm in bed; can't you see the lights are out? Can't you tell the door is closed? I can't get up now I'll wake the children (and my wife will make me pay the price for the next week!)." Luke 11:7.

Jesus explains that the friend will not get up just because it is a friend who is requesting, but because the friend shamelessly persists, he will give him as much as he needs. In a similar way:

"Ask and keep on asking, and it shall be given you; seek and keep seeking, you shall find; knock and keep knocking, and the door shall be opened to you. For every one who asks and keeps on asking received, and he who seeks and keeps on seeking finds, and to him who

knocks and keeps on knocking the door shall be opened!" Luke 11: 9-10, *Amplified Bible.*

Are you beginning to put the puzzle together? This excites me beyond my ability to communicate in pen! This gives me personal hope—but what's more, it gives us hope for our nation!

Time passed but Jesus' lessons on communication did not end. Following the crucifixion, in preparation for His heavenly ascension, Jesus prepared his disciples for the POWER:

"Then He opened their minds so they could understand the Scriptures. He told them, this is what is written: The Christ will suffer and rise from the dead on the third day, and repentance and forgiveness of sins will be preached in His name to all nations, beginning [here at HOME] *in Jerusalem. You are witnesses of these things. I am going to send you what my Father has promised; but stay in the city until you have been clothed with POWER FROM ON HIGH."* Luke 24: 45-49, *New International Version.*

When was this promise fulfilled? The book of Acts and the second chapter gives us a glimpse:

"And when the day of Pentecost had fully come, they were all assembled together in one place. When suddenly there came a sound from heaven like the rushing of a violent tempest blast, and it filled the whole house in which they were sitting. And there appeared to them tongues resembling fire, which were separated and distributed and that settled on each one of them— AND THEY WERE FILLED, diffused throughout their souls—with the Holy Spirit and began to speak in other (different, foreign) languages, as the Spirit kept giving

them clear and loud expression (in each tongue in appropriate words)." Acts 2: 1-4, *Amplified Bible.*

Are you grasping this? Is your heart bursting with new hope? Can you see that the present condition of our society can change when God's people humble themselves and pray and seek His face? Notice that time had passed between the first request of the disciples and the day of Pentecost. There is no doubt that they already had begun to put into practice the teachings of Jesus—they were already beginning to experience the power of prayer. The result of this is hidden in the first part of this verse. It is often overlooked because the magnificence of the entire experience is so overpowering. But here it is. Let it ring in your heart for a moment:

"And when the day of Pentecost had fully come, they were all assembled TOGETHER!" Acts 2:1.

Picture, if you will, the spiritual awakening, the heavenly power to be generated when Christians, God's people, called by His name, take their focus off of themselves and unite with Christian brothers and sisters, in one accord—with singleness of purpose.

Christian, are you experiencing the power of prayer? Is it real to you?

Let me just share a personal experience. As a youngster I had a difficult time understanding prayer. I was actually concerned that I would never find a time when no one else in the world was praying. How could I ever capture the attention of Almighty God with everyone else praying at the same time? I didn't understand the personal relationship He had already established in my life.

One day I allowed my imagination to get involved in my prayer. I actually imagined leaving my room and being translated through the atmosphere to the pearly gates of heaven. I imagined those pearly doors slowly opening to allow my humble entrance. I saw a heavenly mist and a brilliant light rolling down the stairway that greeted me. On my knees, I slowly climbed those stairs until I envisioned the nail-scarred feet of Him who sat upon the throne. I humbly removed my backpack in which I concealed my trials and tribulations, my anguish, my fears, my humble requests. I laid each and every article in my backpack before the Lord and sincerely acknowledged my weakness and His strength. Sounds spiritual enough so far—right?

As I ended my prayer, I began to clear the cluttered staircase of my failures, my guilt, my broken promises, my fears and my needs. I returned each into my backpack just as I had brought them.

AND THEN IT HAPPENED!

In my imagination He who sat upon the throne quietly and lovingly asked: *"Why do you so quickly take back that which you have just entrusted to Me?"*

In that moment I experienced God personally! Friend, you need only to leave the challenges of life there—with Him.

When we recognize ourselves as His people, called by His name, and when we humble ourselves and pray, we are prepared to enjoy His presence, seek His guidance and thereby influence our community, our nation.

AND SEEK MY FACE

Genesis chapter 3 tells the story of the temptation and fall of man. We will review this later in more detail but allow me to draw your attention to verse 8:

"And they [Adam and Eve] heard the voice of the Lord God walking in the garden in the cool of the day: and Adam and his wife hid themselves from the presence of the Lord God among the trees of the garden."

Until this time, Adam and Eve enjoyed open fellowship with God. There was nothing hindering their communion. It was natural; it was good. Sin, however, caused a fatal separation. It is important to note that God did not alter His relationship with man. God, knowing full well what had taken place, still walked through the Garden, just as He always had, in search of communion with those He loved. But Adam and Eve *hid themselves from the presence of the Lord God.*

God still seeks communion with His people. The very term, *"and seek my face"* denotes God's desire for man to enjoy the presence of God. Keep in mind, God does not remove Himself. He keeps his commitment to be present each and every day, ready to commune with His people—as they PRAY and SEEK His FACE.

Perhaps we take our access to Almighty God a bit too casually. In the Old Testament, only the high priest was allowed access to God in the temple—and that, only once a year under strict guidelines. Three very heavy curtains or veils separated the people from the Holy of Holies wherein the Ark of the Covenant was located and where, above the cherubim, the Shekinah Glory abode. Even this word "Shekinah" means "the One Who dwells." We are once again reminded that it is God who initiates His desire to dwell with His people. We enjoy that relationship as we sincerely seek His face.

Within the story of the crucifixion, there is a significant event often missed because of the enormity of the crucifixion itself.

"Jesus, when he had cried again with a loud voice, yielded up the spirit. And behold, the veil of the temple was torn in two from the top to the bottom and the earth did quake and the rocks were split" Matthew 27: 50-51.

Curious isn't it? The veils that separated man from the Almighty were torn in two—and even more significant, they were torn *from top to bottom.* God always takes the first step in fellowship with His people. The tearing of that veil symbolically allowed mankind access to the holy of holies—into the very presence of God. To keep seeking God's face is not a desperate hide-and-go-seek game. It isn't a spiritual scavenger hunt. It is recognizing and enjoying God's originally intended open fellowship with Him. It is standing in His presence, nothing hindering communion. It is natural; it is good.

"But let us, who are of the day, be sober, putting on the breastplate of faith and love, and, for a helmet, the hope of salvation. For God hath not appointed us to wrath but

to obtain salvation by our Lord Jesus Christ, Who died for us that, whether we wake or sleep, we should live together with Him. Wherefore, comfort yourselves together, and edify one another, even as also ye do. And we beseech you brethren, to know them who labor among you, and are over you in the Lord, and admonish you, and to esteem them very highly in love for their work's sake. And be at peace among yourselves. Now we exhort you brethren, warn them that are unruly, encourage the fainthearted, support the weak, be patient toward all men. See that none render evil for evil unto any man, but ever follow that which is good, both among yourselves and to all men. Rejoice evermore! Pray without ceasing! In everything give thanks; for this is the will of God in Christ Jesus concerning you. Quench not the Spirit. Despise not prophesying. Prove all things; hold fast that which is good. Abstain from all appearance of evil. And the very God of peace sanctify you wholly; and I pray your God your whole spirit and soul and body be preserved blameless unto the coming of our Lord Jesus Christ. Faithful is He that calleth you, who will do it!" 1 Thessalonians 5: 8-24.

Once again, all the elements of 2 Chronicles 7:14 are present. Here the Apostle Paul admonishes the "togetherness" of the powerful army of God. He encourages [our] humility as a servant of one another and of Christ, motivates us with the promise of the never ceasing presence of God through prayer. If indeed God has raised up such an army, what could possibly hinder the impact of His army upon our nation?

In battle, there must be a decisive plan for victory. There must be a singleness of purpose, a total commitment to that purpose and the vision of victory as its final outcome. No battle can be won without that united singleness of purpose—leadership and victory demands it! And yet our Bible tells us: *"All we like sheep have gone astray. We have turned every one to his own way, and the Lord hath laid on Him the iniquity of us all."* Isaiah 53: 6.

We have taken a wrong turn. It may be the sin of commission (doing that which is openly against God) or the sin of omission (not doing that which is openly commanded of God).

You may be reading this having reached the end of your rope or you may be a highly lauded seemingly successful and spiritual minister of the Gospel. You may be sincere, but if you are not living in the presence of God, you are SINcerely wrong. If our nation is to experience revival, we must search deep within ourselves and deal with sin.

AND TURN FROM
THEIR WICKED WAYS

The book *In His Steps* made popular a question that has once again become in vogue, "What Would Jesus Do?"—WWJD necklaces, bracelets and pins have made their way to the "altars" of numerous retail stores. Evangelical Christians encourage young people to use this quick and simple tool as a means of governing their actions in determining what is right and what is wrong. WWJD becomes the standard by which the "right" decisions are made.

Simple—right?

So, WHAT WOULD Jesus do? How could anyone possibly divorce themselves from their own personal bias to respond to the question honestly? Talk show hosts ask, "What kind of car would Jesus drive? Would He be a conservative or liberal? How about His living conditions? Frankly, what difference [if any] does it make?"

If Jesus is truly to be considered, we must allow Him to take THE predominant position in our lives. What we *think* He would or wouldn't do must be governed by a greater standard than our own opinions—or else we rationalize and seek our own desire rather than His. If we truly seek Him we must selflessly seek to prove Him true. We must, in our quest, seek to "glorify Him." If His glorification alone is desired, we minimize the temptation to misappropriate His word to simply justify our actions.

As a youngster I remember a popular Christian song whose lyrics were, "Only one life—will soon be past. Only what's done for Christ will last."

I do not intend to create dissension in Christendom. Enough already exists in the Church (ecclesia; body of Christ—believers). But I must ask, "Who actually has a corner on the Christian market? Which 'church' has the inside scoop on the truth?" It is almost taboo for me to exercise such a question—we all know that the church **WE** belong to is right—right?

On the other hand, perhaps dissent results from too much being done in Jesus' name and too little being done for just for Jesus; too much "show" and not enough "share."

Churches and their ministerial staffs are often qualified or validated by the numbers of independent, individualized programs, i.e., "ministries" (often a Christian code for "social gatherings") upon which they have embarked. Many specialized ministries are, at their very core, well intended. Too often, however, they isolate one particular segment of the "body" from fellowship with the corporate body. Gone is the true assembly of believers and therefore diminished is the power of Pentecost, sold out for an entertaining Christianity that is more in vogue with popularity than Pentecostal POWER. The net result is a series of satellite "fellowships" within the local church. And while this may appear to minister to specific and immediate needs (i.e. singles groups, single again groups, thinking about being single again groups, et al) it does not allow the individual to assimilate with the entire church body. It therefore becomes impossible for the individual to function outside of their specific ministry group.

The cycle of isolation is reinforced in the name of ministry. Many a wonderful opportunity for healing, growing and fellowship is missed because "ministries" were allowed to become social orders of commiserating participants. A ministry might be sincere—but sincerely wrong!

This is not only true with special ministries focused upon individuals with special needs in their lives. There is an ever growing trend to shape ministry to specific age groups, social groups, special interests groups and the list goes on. In addition, we have a variety of styles for worship services to meet the needs (in other words, entertainment preferences) of young and old alike.

Pardon my sarcasm but, would it be such an "unbearable situation" if the senior generation and the young parents were no longer isolated from one another by individualized, needs-oriented ministries, but forced to fellowship together from time to time? How, you might ask, could they possibly commiserate? What could they possibly find in common? After all, the seniors have already raised their families—of what use could they possibly be now? What about our youth? Imagine, if you can, the negative impact it would have on a young person allowed to observe their very own parents humbling themselves to the wisdom of the seniors. How could they ever respect their parents again?

What if "ministries" were not simply designed to fill an age-appropriate social calendar, or to please the membership? What if ministries had in mind—just Jesus?

Impossible!

First, we would have to wait for the denominational offices to print new literature. We would have to elect a planning committee. But WHAT NIGHT COULD THEY POSSIBLY MEET? How many should we elect? Will there be enough men, women, and minorities represented? Will they agree with us? How do we organize the next six weeks' sermons so that the messages progressively shape the will of the congregation into compliance? POSTERS! WE NEED POSTERS! We'll get the youth to print the posters and the Music Ministry Team to put together a jingle! That's it—a jingle! We will put it on a transparency and sing it over and over again during the morning worship service until its tune and lyric are so imbedded in our minds one would think they just disembarked Disneyland's "Small World."

Of course, segregated groups offer the pastor a greater degree of job security. By segregating "ministries" there is little opportunity for the corporate body to actually unite on anything! Therefore, if the Singles event wasn't a hit last weekend, no problem; the Over-Seventy fellowship should offer enough political ballast to steady the ship. (Besides, keep the ones with expendable cash happy—right?)

So, what is our motive? Better yet, WHO is our motivation? Successful living, with *eternity's values in view*, is the result of a life grounded and committed to just Jesus. But where is He? He is often spoken of in the past tense, sometimes in the future tense—but seldom in the present tense. Where is He NOW? What is He doing right NOW? What difference will he make in my life NOW?

There is one certainty: Jesus is Who He is regardless of the opinions of any religious leaders or organizations. Who He is does not begin or cease to be as the result of someone's theology. Who He is, is not affected by the exegesis of religious scholars. The amalgamation of all the theological and literary genius ever to walk the earth cannot impact Who He is. For Jesus must eternally be Who He eternally has been and Who He eternally is. He is the first and last, beginning and end, alpha and omega—or He is a liar and a phony; the main character, willingly or not, in the greatest hoax perpetrated upon humanity. **A choice must be made**.

For the Christian, ultimate and eternal authority rests only in Jesus. Perhaps you have a desire to know the deeper meaning of the Word of God—this is good. Now you must ask yourself if there is an equal desire to live the clear, simple and humble life proclaimed by the Person of focus in its pages.

If the truth were known, each of us too often responds to people and circumstances in a pseudo-spiritual manner for self-gain rather than for the glorification of Jesus. Although I am drawn to God's Word, I must resist the desire to simply robe myself in the appearances of being knowledgeable. What is my motive? Is it sincere and spiritual or is it manipulative and self-edifying? Do I sincerely seek to edify Jesus from a truly broken and humble spirit or is it out of compulsion—knowing that by presenting such a façade I might more easily win the social praise of my fellow Christians? Hey, maybe even sell a book?

God is not a concept. If He were, specificity and absolutes would not exist. There could be no Divine guidance. The Ten Commandments might just as well be considered the "Ten Suggestions." Relativity reigns and relationship retires. Eat drink and be merry, for tomorrow you die. Or as the 1970s song asked, "Is that all there is?" No, God is not a concept. Creation's opinion of God does not by any means alter the reality, sovereignty and very essence of God. A debate as it pertains to the existence of a Greater Being to Whom the general public refers to in one way or another as "god or God" is sadly humorous. Unless spiritual existence does not itself exist, at some point in eternity, creation will come face to face with the Truth. If, however, creation is a pointless mass of ever-converging chemical and atomic action and reaction, then [again] there is little use for this discussion—("...if that's all there is..."). May I have the next dance?

THE ORIGINAL SIN

The original sin, as described in the book of Genesis, brought about cataclysmic results. Man's relationship with God had been broken. If the truth were known, it was not man's infatuation with the fruit that created his fall from grace. Nor can Eve carry all the responsibility for man's fall. Man was infatuated with the potential of being a god. He would know good and evil—thus, as the serpent tempted, he would be just like God. Once God's command was breached, there was no human means of turning back! Man's relationship with God had been broken. Certainly if it were possible for Adam and Eve to redeem themselves they would have. When they made aprons from leaves to hide their nakedness, it was not the nakedness of their bodies that shamed them. It was the nakedness of their rebellion before an Almighty God that caused them shame. Their attempts, however sincere, were, once again, SINcerely wrong—they knew it!

Notice, they did not seek God—they attempted to hide from Him. It was He who sought His own. Man's provision for himself (Genesis 3:7) fell short of God's redemption. As a result, judgment fell upon everything that had been created.

Nothing escaped the judgment of God (Genesis 3:14-19). But God, in His infinite love, chose to make a provision for man. God, for reasons known only to Himself, provided the first blood sacrifice (Genesis 3:21). He clothed man with the coat of innocence (the blood of an innocent animal) so that He could reestablish the lost relationship man could not establish on his own and by himself. God extended His love to man so that while man was still lost and without him, God offered atonement through a blood sacrifice.

Does this scenario sound familiar? We see God's requirement for a blood sacrifice to atone for sin in the story of Israel's flight from Egypt. We see that every home where the blood had been applied above the doors and on the lintel was passed over by the death angel.

My Jewish friends might depart from this writing for the moment. I want to briefly examine the New Testament story of the death of Jesus. Why was it that the Jewish leaders could not condemn Jesus to death? Why did they rush him before Pilate? Simply put, the Jews were preparing for a very important celebration—Passover! The parallels are too obvious to be completely ignored.

Whatever else one might conclude, it must be recognized that this man Jesus, Whom the New Testament claims is the LAMB of God, as prophesized in Isaiah 53, was being prepared for death precisely during the preparation of the Passover wherein a blameless, spotless lamb was being prepared for sacrifice as an atonement for sin. It is curious. Could it possibly be that the original sin and sacrifice of atonement were once and for all completed at Calvary? **A choice must be made.**

I've digressed. Let's return to the topic. How does the Christian determine right from wrong? If the opinion of the Christian majority is to be considered the barometer by which right and wrong are determined, what governs the majority? What is it that provides a constant? If truth is considered to be relative, governed only by that which the majority believes to be true under certain circumstances, there is no recognized absolute [authority] from which to choose a direction in accordance with, or in opposition to, life's circumstances. But truth is not relative. Jesus said: *"I am the way the TRUTH and the life; no man cometh unto the Father, but by me."* John 14:6.

No, my friend, there is no grading on a curve. God's standard is perfection—and every man falls short. Jesus made a way for us through His death, burial and resurrection. He was clearly aware of His calling when the words of John 14:6 were spoken. The veils of the temple were torn from top to bottom in an outward expression of this spiritual victory. Our spiritual victory awaits us. Our nation desperately needs us. God's love compels us. Christ's death enables us. The Spirit's enlightening empowers us. Romans 8:37, 38 identify us!

"Nay in all these things we are more than conquerors through Him that loved us. For I am persuaded that neither death, nor life, nor angels, nor principalities, nor powers, nor things present, nor things to come, nor

height, nor depth, nor any other creation, shall be able to separate us from the love of God which is in Christ Jesus our Lord!"

A family enjoys harmony when each member recognizes their individual responsibility and unselfishly contributes; so too the spiritual family of God. The variety of talents and personalities within our spiritual family help not only to broaden an appreciation for one another but to also strengthen the whole.

When united in a singularity of purpose, our spiritual family unit is impregnable, immovable, unshakable, unstoppable and unbeatable. Sin separates us from the fellowship we are admonished to seek, but what is it that woos us back? Is it "really" the continual reminder from the pulpit of our unworthiness—the dirtiness of our unseen actions, thoughts, desires; the putrid stench of our sinfulness to the nostrils of Almighty God? Or has Satan's counterfeit disease of chronic guilt replaced the redeeming healing of God's genuine loving conviction? Are continual heavy doses of condemnation the appropriate medicine for the soul or might it too often drive us away from the Mighty Healer of body, mind and soul? Have we minimized His love for us? Think about it. If sinfulness is keeping you from your God, perhaps you don't need to focus so much upon how big your sin is. Perhaps you need to focus on how much bigger your God is. Let Him know you recognize it. That is what confession is—being in agreement with God about your sin and doing something about it! He has already paid its price!

Congregations tend to pressure ministerial staff members to "grow big churches." Some appear to believe that the proof of spirituality is in the numbers of people on the Sunday school roster, the square footage of the sanctuary, the number of services on a Sunday morning, and the size of the parking lot! We all know that true spirituality is determined by the color of the choir robes and carpet—right?

I actually served in a local church where such a groundswell of opposition arose. At a church business meeting, a disgruntled member stood and blasted her hostility towards the staff: "Numbers! Numbers! Numbers! We need more NUMBERS!" To add some modicum of credibility to her tirade, she further proclaimed, "Even God was interested in NUMBERS and named a Book of the Bible after it!"

Big church, small church, local church, home church, what is the message and the motivation? I hardly think Jesus would have been rated as spiritually successful if He were held to such a barometer. We only know of a handful that actually followed Him. One of them had him arrested and the others forsook Him. So, was He a failure?

As mentioned previously, the temptation is ever present to take one's eye off of the ministry of Christ only to replace it with the "marketing" of Christ. It appears to me that the psychology of sales and marketing has, in some instances, replaced an honest concern for people, an honest desire to introduce them to the Savior so that they too might personally know Him. Marketing schemes and trick questions designed to trap the unsuspecting victim by their own words are being utilized to snare these vulnerable individuals and therefore build mega-organizations loosely known as "churches." Once assimilated, this organization requires the leadership of a large business corporation. Order is required. Order requires conformity—not necessarily an independent freedom to be whom God has called an individual to be. Oh, don't get me wrong, they can be whom God intended as long as it conforms to the spiritual guidelines established by the chosen spiritual hierarchy of that particular local church. Can you see why this makes me a little nervous? Where is God's direction derived; from the pulpit alone? Does it come from those chosen few "spiritual parishioners" who just happen to also be the church's greater financiers?

I realize my comments pertaining to mega-church organizations seem harsh. I do not intend this. I hope to encourage local church leadership to take personal inventory examining their personal motives and bathing each and every ministry or decision in hours of selfless prayer. I pray that each member of the local body asks whether or not the ministry is just for Jesus. Is it a selfless ministry of love, the sacrificial desire for the community in which it is located, or is it in competition with the church down the street? Is it to increase the roll thereby increasing the income to continue to perpetuate "good ministries?" Are we building a social enterprise or are we participating with Christ Jesus in the completion of His Church?

The Apostle John, while exiled on the island of Patmos, penned the following words: *"And to the angel (messenger) of the assembly (the church) in Laodicea write: These are the words of the Amen, the trusty and faithful and true Witness, the Origin and Beginning and Author of God's creation. I know your [record of] works and what you are doing; you are neither cold nor hot. Would that you were cold or hot! So, because you are lukewarm, and neither cold nor hot, I will spew you out of My mouth! For you say, I am rich, I have prospered and grown wealthy, and I am in need of nothing; and do not realize and understand that you are wretched, pitiable, poor, blind and naked. Therefore I counsel you to purchase from Me gold refined and tested by fire, that you may be [truly] wealthy, and white clothes to clothe you and to keep the shame of your nudity from being seen, and salve to put on your eyes that you may see. Those whom I [dearly and tenderly] love, I tell their faults and convict and convince and reprove and chasten— [that is,] I discipline and instruct them. So be enthusiastic and in earnest and burning with zeal, and repent— changing your mind and attitude. Behold I stand at the door and knock; if any one hears and listens to and heeds My voice and opens the door, I will come in to him and will eat with him, and he [shall eat] with Me."* Revelation 3:14-20.

There are many in our spiritual family who have unceremoniously exiled themselves from fellowship with a local church body. They feel the pressure to conform to the image of the local church rather than be transformed by the renewing of their mind to become more Christ-like. As a result, they become sensitized to ministries preaching the message of conformity rather than transformation. They were motivated by what their Christian brothers and sisters thought until they realized, most of them don't! These well-meaning brothers and sisters had simply conformed to the rationale of the local body without ever personally considering who God had created them to be.

"Cookie-cutter Christians! Holiday special! Collect them all! The same image, the same message, the same mess. How about a new message? How about one that confesses, 'I haven't got the faintest idea what's going on. I don't have all of the answers and I don't feel the need to have them. I am depending upon God Almighty to shoot straight with a crooked stick! I am still a work in progress!'"

Conform, conform, conform! Do this or else! What if the prophets of old conformed rather than trans-formed? How would it have affected the ministry of Moses and the Old Testament prophets? How would it have impacted the ministry of the Apostles Paul, Peter and John and the writers of the New Testament?

Where in the world are the Christians who are willing to stand for something and not fall for anything? Where are His people who are willing to shamelessly express His love through a humble life that prayerfully seeks God's face, acknowledges sin, turns from their own way? Where are those who are in communication with God?

Our struggle against self-will is real. It was real for the Apostle Paul who wrote:

"For I do not understand my own actions—I am baffled, bewildered. I do not practice or accomplish what I wish, but I do the very thing that I loathe [which my moral instinct condemns]. Now if I do [habitually] what is contrary to my desire, [that means that] I acknowledge

*and agree that the Law is good (morally excellent) and that I take sides with it. However, it is no longer I who do the deed, but the sin [principle] which is at home in me and has possession of me. For I know that nothing good dwells within me, that is in my flesh. I can will what is right, but I cannot perform it! I have the intention and the urge to do what is right, but no power to carry it out. For I fail to practice the good deeds I desire to do, but the evil deeds, that I do not desire to do are what I am [ever] doing. Now if I do what I do not desire to do, it is no longer I doing it—it is not myself that acts—but the sin [principle] which dwells within me [fixed and operating in my soul]. So I find it to be a law [of my being] that when I want to do what is right and good, evil is ever present with me and I am subject to its insistent demands. O unhappy and pitiable and wretched man that I am! Who will release and deliver me from [the shackles of] this body of death? O thank God He Will! Through Jesus Christ, the Anointed One, our Lord! So then indeed I, of myself with the mind and heart serve the Law of God, **but with the flesh the law of sin**.* " Romans 7:15-21; 25-25.

Somehow I find a bit of solace knowing that even Paul wrestled within himself. And yet, as sinful as Paul saw himself to be he could also write:

"Yes, furthermore I count everything as loss compared to the possession of the priceless privilege—the overwhelming preciousness, and surpassing worth and supreme advantage—of knowing Christ Jesus my Lord, and progressively becoming more deeply and intimately acquainted with Him, of perceiving and recognizing and understanding Him more fully and clearly. For His sake I have lost everything and consider it all to be mere

rubbish (refuse, dregs), in order that I may actually win (gain) Christ, the Anointed One. And that I may [actually] be found and known as in Him, not having any (self-achieved) righteousness that can be called my own, based upon my obedience to the Law's demands—ritualistic uprightness and [supposed] right standing with God thus acquired—but possessing that [genuine righteousness] which comes through faith in Christ the Anointed One, the [truly] right standing with God, which comes from God by (saving) faith. [For my determined purpose is] that I may know Him—that I may progressively become more deeply and intimately acquainted with Him, perceiving and recognizing and understanding [the wonders of His Person] more strongly and more clearly. And that I may in that same way come to know the power out-flowing from His resurrection [which it exerts over believers] and that I may so share His sufferings as to be continually transformed [in spirit into His likeness even] to His death [in the hope] that if possible I may attain to the [spiritual and moral] resurrection [that lifts me] out from among the dead [even while in the body]. Not that I have now attained [this ideal] or am already made perfect, but I press on to lay hold of (grasp) and make my own, that for which Christ Jesus, the Messiah, has laid hold of me and made me His own. I do not consider, brethren, that I have captured and made it my own [yet]; but one thing I do—it is my one aspiration: forgetting what lies behind and straining forward to what lies ahead, I press on toward the goal to win the [supreme and heavenly] prize to which God in Christ Jesus is calling us upward."
Philippians 3:8-14.

This passage speaks for itself but please allow me to make one very important point, Christian brothers and sisters. It is a simple point—perhaps overlooked at a first glance. Please focus with me upon the statement: *"Forgetting what lies behind and straining forward to what lies ahead..."*

So often this small phrase has been translated, "forgetting about past failures, I press forward to greater successes." This is not an inaccurate translation but I fear it is an incomplete translation. Allow me to share a personal story with you.

As young boy, I ran on my high school track team. I wasn't a stand-out but I did compete and place enough to gain points for my team. My accumulated points allowed me to participate in the North Coast Trials. This was a thrill because I needed only to place to be awarded the opportunity to race in the televised finals!

My excitement was quickly quelled when I heard that I would be running in a heat with California's fastest 440 sprinter. I committed myself to work harder than ever before. I beat my body into submitting to the task at hand; the reward of victory was greater than the pain of preparation! As the day of the heat approached, I was with singular mind, focused upon my chest hitting that finish line before anyone! I owned that race!

The day finally arrived. I was ready. I was totally prepared. I was focused and positive. My spikes were the proper length, the temperature was perfect, the track was impeccable. I slowly and deliberately got into the starting blocks. The lanes were staggered, thus giving the impression that those in the furthest lane out had a shorter distance to run. I was in lane one; my opponent, lane three.

One last glance forward allowed me to convince myself that he was already ahead and I had to dig deep into the reservoir of commitment and training to expend every ounce of strength just to catch up. The gun went off and I exploded out of the blocks. The nervous energy that had welled within me burst through my legs and arms like never before. The moment I heard that gun I was already straining forward for the tape 440 yards ahead! As I made that last turn the truth of the race was made evident. I was at least twenty yards in front of the field—I WON!

Immediately after the race I thought to myself, *That really wasn't too hard.* I had energy to spare. My opponent wasn't all that fast.

Having so decimated my opponent (and those in our heat) my preparation for finals (the following weekend) was less intense. I basked in the thrill of victory. I could foresee myself on television at the top of the podium, first place!

When the gun sounded at finals, I saw nothing but my opponents heels vanishing into the distance. I lost the race. I lost the race miserably. I was in total shock—who was this guy? Where did he come from and why wasn't he here the week before? I later found out that my opponent had been suffering from a very serious case of the flu the week before, but he had been equally determined to run the race.

My reason for this story? As important as it is to forget our past failures when we run the spiritual race set before us, it is equally important that we not relax on our past victories. The spiritual opposition never rests. It is in a constant race for the soul of our nation. Forget the past victories. It is important that we fervently prepare ourselves daily for the race at hand. We cannot rest upon the victory of yesterday—we must be prepared for the race set before us today! Are you ready?

There are the sins of transgressing the law of God (sins of commission) and the sins of not transmitting the love of God, doing what we know we should do (sins of omission).

"To him that knoweth to good and doeth it not, to him it is sin." James 4:17.

Sin is SIN, sin is wrong and sin separates us from the presence of God. It is evil, abhorrent—and it is the one thing we all have in common. No wonder we so often enjoy it together. We don't want to see it as abhorrent. We would rather classify sin in degrees or focus upon those sins WE are not prone to do. That's why the writer of the book of Hebrews knocks the stilts out from under us when he talks about specific sins that separate us from fellowship with God (and since they are not necessarily sins I enjoy—no problem) and adds: *"...let us lay aside every weight, and the sin which doth so easily beset us..."* Hebrews 12:1.

So, what is your pet sin? What is it that so easily besets YOU? What is it that keeps you from seeking God's face? Acknowledge it, be in agreement with God about your sin and do something about it! He has already paid its price!

THEN WILL I HEAR FROM HEAVEN AND WILL FORGIVE THEIR SIN AND WILL HEAL THEIR LAND

Paul, in his letter to the church at Philippi writes: *"Rejoice in the Lord always—delight, gladden yourselves in Him; again I say, Rejoice! Let all men know and perceive and recognize your unselfishness—your considerateness, your forbearing spirit. The Lord is near—He is coming soon! Do you fret or have any anxiety about anything, but in every circumstance and in everything by prayer and petition [definite requests] with thanksgiving continue to make your wants known to God."* Philippians 4:4-6.

What does God want for us? What does any parent want for their child? Maybe a starting point is, God wants us to be happy. This verse is not a passive suggestion; it is a loving command. **Rejoice!** God wants us to be able to live each and every moment in anticipation of the next.

The irony is found in the fact that the very elements of 2 Chronicles 7:14 are also the very elements resulting in the joy of our salvation. It is being that man, woman or child of God humbly accessing the throne of grace through prayer; enjoying the peace that passes all understanding in the presence of God; being free from the clenches of habitual sin and knowing its debt was paid, once and for all, by our loving Savior. Finally, it is the certainty that God hears us; He cares; He is present, available and waiting to fellowship with us!

Perhaps you are not a Christian; *good for you!* It is best to be honest about it. Having therefore been honest, what motivated you to read this little booklet? No doubt you are like everyone else—searching. Don't buy into a façade your unsaved [or for that matter your holier-than-thou Christian] friends are erecting.

What is **your personal relationship with God right now?**

Why not settle it right now? Why wait any longer? Why miss the blessing?

"How do I do it?" you ask. There are many ways that seem logical to people but those end in emptiness and destruction. There are really only two religions in the world. There is the religion that says a person must in some way do something to earn their way to heaven, and there is the religion that simply depends upon what one Man did for all who will believe. That man is Jesus. He paid the price once and for all so that if anyone will accept Him—that is to say, willingly give their life to His care and keeping—He will come to them and fellowship with them forever! Sounds too simple, right? But why would a loving God allow pain and suffering? Why do good people suffer, children die? I don't know.

I do know this—good people and evil people suffer alike. The only difference is that the Christian need not go through the woes of this world alone; therein is comfort and peace.

Christian, it is time to get moving; even God cannot steer a parked car! **It is time to wise up, o man of God! It is time to wise up—and rise up!** It is time to allow God's majesty and awesome power to be seen against the billowing clouds of the coming storm. It is time to give Him the reins and let Him direct the message! This is a call to arms! There IS VICTORY on the horizon. While the tempestuous waves of sin break upon the Solid Rock, the Rock stands firm—and those who will rise up upon the Rock of Ages will impact this nation!

"Therefore then, since we are surrounded by so great a cloud of witnesses [who have borne testimony of the Truth], let us strip off and throw aside every encumbrance—unnecessary weight—and that sin which so readily (deftly and cleverly) clings to and entangles us, and let us run with patience endurance and steady and active persistence the appointed course of the race that is set before us. Looking away [from all that will distract] to Jesus, Who is the Leader and the Source of our faith [giving the first incentive for our belief] and is also its Finisher, [bringing it to maturity and perfection]. He, for the joy [of obtaining the prize] that was set before Him, endured the cross, despising and ignoring the shame, and is now seated at the right hand of the throne of God." Hebrews 12:1-2.

CONCLUSION

The future of America depends upon the spiritual condition of God's people. Who are they? They are truck drivers, engineers, students, and clergy. They are actors, carpenters and computer technicians. They are bikers, scientists, housewives, attorneys, and musicians. They are young and gregarious. They are old, often feeble and alone.

There are no statues to commemorate their deeds, no oil paintings of them to decorate the great halls of government. They may not be remembered by historians but they, YOU, are essential to the revival of our nation.

The time for personal revival is now. The time for commitment is now but commitment is no easy task; you have to stick with it!

Commitment is the consistent pursuit of a specific goal. Commitment is pouring one's self into a specific task, emptying oneself of all other objectives and focusing, with singleness of purpose, upon one specific endeavor. There is no stopping, slowing or turning. Commitment is the underlying focal point of every moment until its objective has been squarely met, challenged and overcome. Commitment separates common endeavor from driven pursuit. No excuse can attach itself to commitment; commitment is never found, "under the circumstances."

Commitment is separated from success only by time and effort. There is no uncertainty in commitment. Once committed to, the task is as good as completed. It is relentless.

Commitment is deaf to the cajoling of the jealous, the prayers of the pious, and the doubts of the defeated. It is blind to danger; there can be no failure. It scorns adversity, embraces risk. There is no obstacle, no natural disaster that can derail true commitment. Commitment faces the impossible and proclaims, "I will not be denied!" Don't give me statistics; don't give me odds; don't give me history; don't give me facts; give me commitment! No other endeavor of mankind can yield eternal value!

The great evangelist D. L. Moody said, "The World has yet to see what God can do with a man fully consecrated [committed] to Him."

Not everyone is in a full-time Christian ministry; however, every Christian is either a missionary or a mission field!

D. L. Moody went on to say, "My citizenship is in heaven, but right now I vote in Cook County."

Years ago, Senator Mark Hatfield wrote, "Our nation's foremost need is the recovery of a relevant moral conscience. Ultimately, that can only be done through individuals, not by the state."

President Coolidge once said, "America was born in a revival of religion." Religious leaders were midwives in helping bring this nation to birth. Involvement in political life continued throughout the years—both inside and outside the church, and in many forms. Look closely at our coins. The work of M.R. Watkinson, a pastor in Ridleyville, Pennsylvania, produced the inscriptions, "Liberty" and "In God We Trust." A Baptist clergyman, Samuel Francis Smith, wrote our great patriotic hymn, "My Country, 'Tis of Thee," in 1832. Another minister, Francis Bellamy, wrote "The Pledge of Allegiance" to the flag in 1892.

What can you do? Well, what do you do; what do you do well? How can you do it, right now, for the cause of Christ? Whatever it is, DO IT! DO WHATEVER IS IN FRONT OF YOU TO DO!

If my simple words have inspired you, if they have caused you to see that this nation is counting upon you and others like you, if it causes you to drop to your knees in prayer for our nation, for divine forgiveness and blessing, then it simply shows how God can still work through His imperfect people. This little book is in vain without the touch and blessing of Almighty God upon your heart and soul.

The call of God is not political, denominational or cultural. It is to every common sinner who humbles himself or herself, prays, seeks God's face and turns from their wicked ways to His way. He hears, He has forgiven, and He will heal our land.